This book belongs to

....

My best friends are

....

....

"There are big ships and small ships but there are no ships like friendships."

Published by Ladybird Books Ltd.
A Penguin Company
Penguin Books Ltd., 80 Strand, London WC2R ORL
Penguin Books Australia Ltd., Camberwell, Victoria, Australia
Penguin Group (NZ), cnr Airborne and Rosedale Roads,
Albany, Auckland 1310, New Zealand

2 4 6 8 10 9 7 5 3 1

Printed in China

Things to Make and Do

Cutie Catcher

Make a special cutie catcher – or fortune teller – that tells you which Disney Cutie you all are!

You'll need:

 a square piece of paper, with sides about 20cm

 coloured pens or crayons

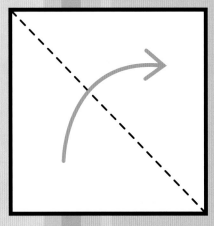

1 Fold the paper in half, corner to corner, to make a triangle.

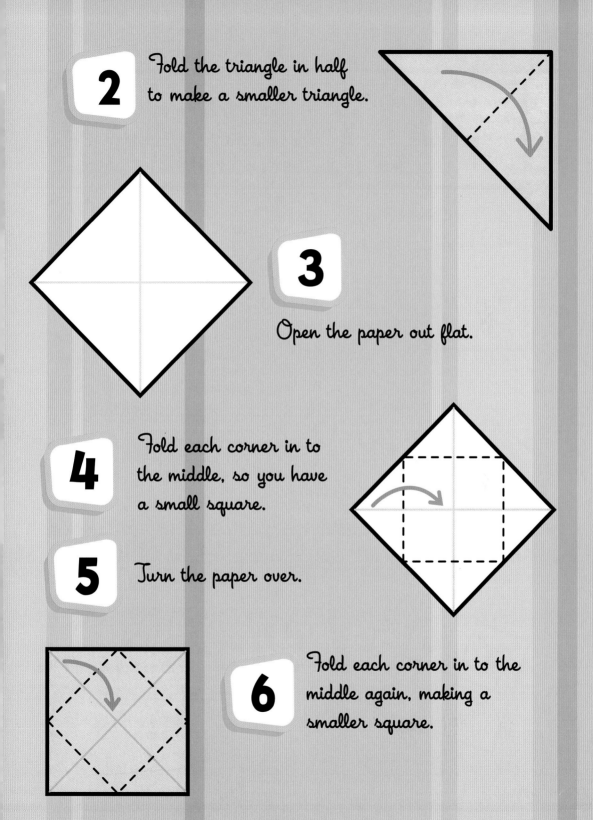

2 Fold the triangle in half to make a smaller triangle.

3 Open the paper out flat.

4 Fold each corner in to the middle, so you have a small square.

5 Turn the paper over.

6 Fold each corner in to the middle again, making a smaller square.

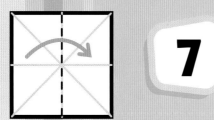

7 Without turning it over, fold the square in half with the top surface inside.

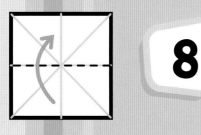

8 Unfold it, and fold it in half the other way. Unfold it again.

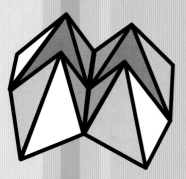

9 On one side, there are four square flaps. Lift these outwards, folding the fortune teller away from you, so that you can put a finger under each flap and move the fortune teller in and out.

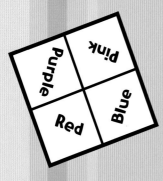

10 Flatten the fortune teller again. Write the name of a colour on each square flap.

11 Turn it over. Write a number on each small triangle – there should be eight.

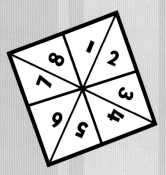

12 Open the triangular flaps outwards and draw a Disney Cutie on each small triangle.

To use the Cutie catcher, put your fingers under the flaps and hold the Cutie catcher closed.

Ask a friend to choose one of the colours on the outside. Move the Cutie catcher in and out for each letter as you spell the colour.

Ask them to choose a number. Move it in and out as you count out the number.

Ask them to choose another number. Look under the flap to see which Cutie they are!

Sweet Dreams

Put on your PJs and snuggle into your sleeping bags for a perfect sleepover.

Dreamy themes

Give your sleepover a theme. It could be something topical, like Halloween or a summer barbecue. Or how about

✿ on the beach

✿ disco divas

✿ movie queens

✿ your favourite TV show.

Make themed invitations and certificates.

Snack attack

* Popcorn and fizzy drinks
* Pizza and salad
* Hot dogs, toffee apples, gob-stopper eyeballs and witchy cakes for a Halloween feast
* Toasted marshmallows and hot chocolate under the stars if you're camping out

Don't forget

* Clothes for the next day
* Toothbrush and toothpaste
* Your favourite snuggly blanket
* Snacks for your midnight feast
* CDs and DVDs
* A little present for the host's mum – make her feel appreciated

Party Games

For a sleepover, a party, or just hanging out together on a rainy day, giggle your way through these easy party games.

"I took... to the party!"

You don't need anything for this game - except friends and imagination!

☆ Imagine you're having a party. It has a secret theme which only one person knows.

☆ That person starts. She says two things she will take to the party. (They don't have to be things you could really take.)

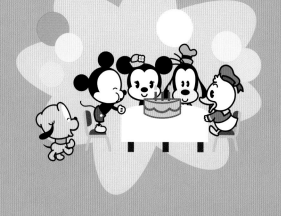

☆ They must both be connected to the theme in some way. So if the theme is green things, she might take a frog and some peas.

☆ The next person, trying to guess the theme, says two things she'll take. The first person says whether she's allowed in or not.

☆ Only one thing has to match the theme. So if the next person said she'd take a rabbit and a carrot, she wouldn't get it. If she said a rabbit and a cucumber, she would.

Go round three times, then take it in turn to say what you think the theme could be.

"I took a bicycle wheel and a beach ball to the party!"

"I took a plate and a box to the party!"

"You can go."

"I took a book and a mug to the party!"

"You can't go."

The theme here is things that are round.

Truth or Dare

You'll need:

* ❀ a die

* ❀ some paper

* ❀ some pens or pencils

You're going to take it in turns to throw the die. If you get six, you have to do a dare or tell the truth. You can choose which to do.

It's best to think of all your dares and questions first and write them on pieces of paper, then someone pulls one out at random when it's needed.

DARE Sing a Christmas carol

TRUTH What's the most embarrassing thing you've done in the last year?

TRUTH What pet name do your mum and dad call you?

DARE Turn all your clothes inside out and wear them like that for the rest of the day

Friendship Consequences

Make wacky things happen to each other!

You'll need:

* strips of paper, about 10cm wide and 30cm long

* a pen or pencil

Sit in a circle. Take a piece of paper each. At the top of the piece of paper, write the name of one of your friends. Don't let anyone see what you've written. Fold over the top of the paper so that the name's hidden, and pass it to the person on your left.

Without looking at the name, each write down 'met up with' and then another name. This time it can be anyone - a friend, a film star or even a character from a book or movie.

Fold the top over and pass the paper on again.

Next, write down where they met. Fold the paper and pass it on again. Then write what they did. When you've finished, pass the paper one last time and take it in turns to open and read out the consequences.

Pooh

met up with Piglet

at the beach

they had a snowball fight

they ate toffee apples

and sandwiches

In Step

Get ready for the next school disco by making up a great dance routine.

Put on one of your favourite tracks and work out some moves together and practise, practise, practise, until every step is perfect.

Dress up in your best disco outfit to make sure you can still do the moves. No point making up a routine you can only do in your pyjamas!

Making Tracks

While you're in a musical mood, put together a tape or CD of all your favourite tracks.

Sing-a-long

Make your very own karaoke tape. Put on a CD track you like and all sing along. Practise a few times, then record it. You can even record it on your mobile and use it as your ringtone!

If some of you play instruments, you can even skip the CD and play and sing as your very own band.

Special songs

Make a special CD of music you like. You can use the computer to copy songs from CDs you've bought, or you can download tracks from the web – there are lots of sites where you can get free songs from bands that are starting out and give their music away for free.

Picture It

It's lovely to have photos of all your friends. Make a special friendship photo album.

Snap happy

Buy a disposable camera - or even one each - and spend a whole day taking photos of each other. You can pick a normal school day, or a special day in the holidays or at the weekend.

Develop your photos and make up a special album of your day. You could get several sets of prints and make an album each.

Say cheese!

Crowd into a photo booth in a shopping centre and take lots of silly snaps of yourselves all together.

Or take a whole lot of photos with your camera phone or digital camera. Move them to the computer to print out the best ones.

Picture perfect

You don't have to leave your photos as they are. You can add extras to the pictures, too. Use stickers to add angel wings or party hats. Why not add your favourite popstar to your photo?

In The Picture

*Make the most of your photos
by making a great picture frame.*

You'll need:

* thick cardboard

* scissors

* glue or sticky tape

* coloured pens, crayons or paints

* stickers, sticky jewels, sequins, bows, shells – anything pretty to stick on it

★ Cut a rectangle of card bigger
than your picture. If you're
putting several pictures together, arrange
them all on the sheet of card first. To keep
the pictures steady, stick them down.

★ Cut a frame from another piece
of card. Start with a rectangle
slightly bigger than the backing
and then cut one or more holes in it so you
can see the pictures. Don't stick this on yet -
decorate it first.

★ Use paints and crayons to colour
it. Add some glitter if you like.
Stick on all your stickers and bits
and pieces. Then stick the frame onto the
backing so you can see your photos.

T-time

Make special team t-shirts,
or make personalised t-shirts for each other.

You'll need:

* plain t-shirts – white's best if you're going to paint or print on them

* fabric paints or pens

* bows, ribbons, buttons and badges to sew on

You don't need to be a fabulous
artist to make a funky t-shirt – you
just need some imagination! You can
copy a design you like or even just
write random words on your t-shirt.
Or put fabric paint on your hands
and add your hand-prints.

Add beads, ribbons, bows, sequins
and buttons with a few stitches to keep
them in place. If you can't sew neatly,
make a feature of your sewing by
stitching in bold coloured wool.

Fair Weather Friends

Don't spend all your time indoors!
Rain or shine, there's plenty to do outside.

Jump in
puddles.

Jump in
piles of
leaves.

Make a snowman, or have a snowball fight.

If it's a blustery day, fly a kite.

Chill out in the sun (but don't forget the sun-block).

Stop Press

Magazines never have exactly the right mix of articles. So why not make your own?

You'll need:

* paper – big sheets are best as you have to fold the pages in half

* pens, pencils and crayons

* scissors

* glue

We ♥ Disney Cuties

Work out what you're going to put in your magazine and who's going to write each bit. Here are some ideas:

* fantasy interviews with movie stars and pop stars
* horoscopes
* a problem page
* embarrassing moments
* make-over tips
* fashion
* stories and poems

Fold your sheets of paper in half across their longest side and slip them one inside another, like a book. Think of a title and write it across the top of the first page.

Draw up columns on your pages, then write your articles on smaller sheets, cut to fit the spaces. You can write and print your articles on the computer, if you like.

Don't forget to draw pictures to stick in. Or you can print out pictures from the web, or cut some out of old magazines and newspapers.

Beauty Treats

Pool all your make-up and nail colours
and have a beauty session.

Look lovely

Start with a face pack so yummy you could eat it!
Make sure you tie back your hair before you start!
Try one of these:

 Mash a few strawberries with oats and plain
yoghurt

 Mash an apricot or peach with a little yoghurt

 Liquidise an apple with a few teaspoons of
honey and a few mint leaves

(Don't use any ingredients you're allergic to.
It's a good idea to test a bit on your arm a
day or two in advance, to make sure.)

Mix the ingredients together, clean your face, then spread the face pack over your skin. Put slices of cucumber or cold tea bags over your eyes. Leave it all for 10-15 minutes and then wash off.

Helping hands

It's much easier to do someone else's nails than your own. Get a grown-up to help with cutting and filing if you need to, then paint each other's nails. Two or three thin coats of nail varnish will look better than one thick one.

Add stick-on jewels or nail transfers for the perfect finish! Don't forget your toes!

Perfect Polish

Charming Arms

Making and swapping friendship bracelets is a great way to show how much you like each other.

You'll need:

✿ coloured wool or embroidery silk

✿ beads

✿ safety pins

✿ scissors

♥ Cut four different coloured lengths of thread about 180cm. Fold each thread in half. Gather the folded peices together and tie a knot about 10cm from the folded ends.

♥ Use a safety pin to fix the knot to a cushion to keep it still while you work. Spread the threads out, in their pairs.

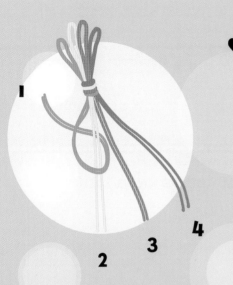

♥ Take the two threads on the left and loop them around the next pair, making a knot. Pull it tight, but not too tight. Repeat this so you have two knots on that pair of threads.

♥ Now tie the same two threads around the next pair. Repeat the knot. Then move on to the next pair of threads. You should have two knots on each of three pairs of threads. The first colour will now be at the right.

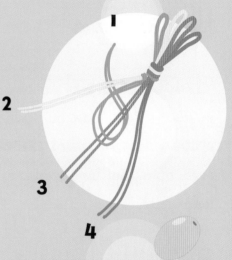

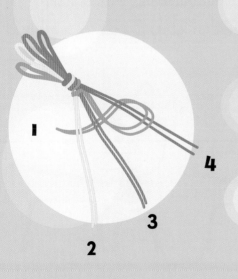

♥ Take the next colour from the left, and use this to make two knots around each of the threads again. Keep going like this until your friendship bracelet is long enough to go round your wrist. Tie a knot at the end. Cut the threads off at about 15cm and tie beads onto the ends. Swap with a friend!

Shhh...

You don't want everyone to know all your secrets - so make up some hidden ways of passing messages!

Nothing there

With invisible ink, no one else even knows you have a message. You can buy invisible ink, or use lemon juice to write with. To reveal the message, heat the paper up - in the oven at a low temperature, or with an iron (ask an adult to help you).

Passing a blank sheet of paper looks suspicious. Put a non-secret message or picture on it as well to stop people wondering what you're doing.

Gobbledegook!

A secret code is a good way of defeating prying eyes.

♥ Letter shift

Move every letter forwards or backwards two or three. In this message, a is shown as c, b as d, and so on.

"Dguv htkgpfu cnycau!"

(Best friends always!)

♥ Secret signs

Every letter has a symbol or picture. You'll need a crib sheet to remind you of what's what! (You can use symbol fonts on the computer to help you.)

Secret handshake

Make up some secret gestures to communicate in a crowded place. Maybe scratching your ear means "Rescue me! I'm bored!", or pretending to sneeze means "Look out, teacher!"

Friendship Flowers

Watch flowers grow as your
friendship grows - aaah, sweet!

Buy a packet of seeds and split it between you. You can
each plant a pot of friendship flowers to grow on your
window sill. This is a great thing to do with a friend who
lives further away - you can send the seeds through the post.

Whose flower is the tallest?

If you buy sunflower seeds, you can have a contest to see who can grow the tallest plant. You won't be able to keep it in a pot – they can grow to two metres!

Mystery Mess

Have a mystery taste and feel session!

You'll need:

❋ a scarf to use as a blindfold

❋ a bowl you can put messy things in

❋ lots of things to taste or feel

Euugh! (It's a great game for Halloween!)

One person chooses things that feel disgusting but are really quite normal. Everyone else takes it in turns to be blindfolded and try to guess what they are, just by touch.

Try:

* tinned spaghetti
* rice pudding
* chopped jelly
* peeled grapes

What could they be? Zombie innards? Eyeballs?

Euugh!

Test you taste buds

How good are you at identifying flavours?
Try guessing mystery flavours - no peeking!

Liquorice?

Sherbet?

Fruits?

Tomato sauce?

Boiled egg white?

Be careful - check no one's allergic to any foods first, and only use things that are real foods. Don't use any meat or fish if there are any vegetarians in your group.

Sticky Stuff

Make a HUGE collage picture together for your wall.

You'll need:

* old magazines
* scissors
* glue
* a very big piece of paper, a roll of wallpaper will do, or large pieces of paper taped together

Gather together all your old magazines and comics and get snipping. Cut out all the best pictures and pile them up.

Then work out how to arrange them all before you start sticking them down. Is there a theme? Do you want to change the colours as you move across the picture? Or will it all be a big jumble?

If you use sticky tack, you can make your collage straight onto the wall. It can grow and grow - add more pictures as you find them, and move around the ones you've got!

A Night at the Movies

If you can't afford to go to the movies,
or there's nothing on that you want to see,
make your own cinema at home!

Stock up on your favourite
DVDs, or rent one you haven't
seen before. Cover the floor with
cushions, get lots of popcorn and
fizzy drinks, or make milkshakes.

Draw the curtains and turn out all the lights so that it's really dark, just like a real cinema.

MOVIE NIGHT
Saturday at 7pm

Drinks and popcorn free!

Design tickets to send out in advance to your friends and make a special evening of it.

What a Doll!

It's lovely to have something a friend's made for you that you can carry around – so why not make friendship dolls for each other?

Use traditional wooden clothes pegs and add scraps of fabric, wool and lace to make dolls that look like each other. Draw on the faces with felt-tip pens.

It's easy to make soft dolls from fabric stuffed with wool or padding. Or get old dolls from a jumble sale and customise them.

Don't worry!

Worry dolls are tiny dolls that you tell your problems to, then slip under your pillow at night. The doll is supposed to do the worrying for you, leaving you free to sleep easily! A doll made by a friend makes a perfect worry doll - it's just like sharing a problem with your friend.

Wardrobe Make-over

If you're bored with your clothes but can't afford anything new, swap and share with friends and customise what you've got.

Make sure... You ask an adult for permission to do this before you start!

Mix 'n' match

Get all your clothes together and try on everything from everyone. It's fun even if you don't end up swapping, as you always know what to borrow to put together a great outfit.

New looks for old

Be creative! Jazz up a plain t-shirt by stitching on ribbons, buttons and patches, or just covering it with badges.

Trousers that are too short can be cropped to shorts. A t-shirt that's shrunk can have new life as a crop-top.

3

Cover holes with bright patches or just pin the edges together with safety pins for a punk look.

Piece of Cake

Make a big cake or pizza to share
and decorate it together.

Pizza factory

Buy or make a pizza base and collect
the toppings you all like. You can use cheese,
mushrooms, ham, pineapple, onion or anything you
like. Spread a thin layer of tomato purée on first,
then take it in turns to decorate your portion of pizza
- a third each for three
of you, a quarter if there's
four of you, and so on.
Don't forget which is
your portion. Remember
it will look slightly
different when
it's cooked.

Ask a grown-up
to put your pizza into
a hot oven for 10-15
minutes until it is
cooked.

Nice slice

Ask an adult to help you make this sponge cake. Make sure it is thoroughly cooled before you decorate it.

Recipe
110g Butter
110g Caster Sugar
110g Self-raising Flour
2 Eggs
2 drops Vanilla Essence

Preheat oven to 190°C: 375°F: Gas 5.

Whisk together the butter and sugar until light and creamy.

Add the beaten eggs gradually with a little of the flour.

Fold in the remaining sieved flour and add the flavouring.

Divide equally between two 15cm sandwich tins.

Bake for 20 - 25 minutes.

Turn out on to a wire rack to cool.

Make a big bowl of white icing and divide into portions so you have at least one portion each. Make sure you have lots of food colouring and decorations to put on the top. Then take it in turns to decorate a share of the cake.

Once Upon A Time...

...a group of friends made up a fabulous story. Write a story together, passing it on from one to the next to add a bit.

Plan ahead

Decide how to divide the work. How much will you each write? A paragraph? A page? How many times will it go round? Are you going to decide the plot in advance or just see what happens? Work out who's going to go next at each point.

✳ Take turns

One of you starts, then passes the story
on after doing the agreed amount. After the
next chunk, it's passed on again.

You can work on paper or on the computer –
email the story from one to another, if you're
not all around at the same time.

✳ Worth a thousand words?

If you don't want to write so much, make a
comic strip story instead – or even just a
big picture that tells a story.

Outdoor Fun

Don't stay cooped up inside all day - get some fresh air and exercise!

Hopscotch

Use pavement chalks to draw on the floor and walls outside. Don't worry - it will all wash away in the rain.

For a bit of bouncing around, draw a hopscotch grid.

Make sure... You are careful near water and always tell an adult where you are going!

Scooter Slalom

Set up a scooter slalom. Place obstacles like flower-pots and buckets and chalk a route around them. See who can do it quickest on their scooter or rollerblades. (Don't forget your padding and helmet - be careful!)

Pooh Sticks

If you've got a river nearby, have a game of Pooh sticks. Each pick a stick - or make a paper boat. Count down to drop them in the river from one side of a foot bridge and see which gets to the other side first. Don't do it where there's traffic. If there's no footbridge, pick markers on the bank - first past the mark wins.

By The Book

Make a friendship scrapbook
together - you can keep adding to it, and
look back through it in future years.

You'll need:

* a scrapbook or a big notebook
* scissors
* glue
* pens
* photos and mementoes

Divide the book into sections with one for each
of you and a final section 'all together'.

In each friend's section, stick photos of her, draw pictures of her favourite things, and stick in mementoes of special times and events. Add nice notes about her and record funny things she's said.

There's nothing like a gal pal!

Daisy's great to go shopping with!

Minnie xx

In the last section, record fun times you spend together and put photos of the whole group of you. Keep tickets and receipts from your outings. Record your special catchphrases and your dreams for the future.

If friends were flowers, I'd pick you!

Pluto's always around to make me smile!

Mickey x

Mate Magnets

Funny magnets are great to stick on the fridge and hold up notes and cards. It's even better to see a friendly face smiling at you from the fridge door!

You'll need:

* sticky-backed magnet sheets
* photos of friends
* scissors

Cut out photos of your friends and peel the backing off a magnet sheet so that you can stick them down. Using scissors, cut the magnet sheet to just the right shape around the photo.

For a special gift, make magnets of a friend's favourite pet, movie star or band - you can cut pictures from magazines.

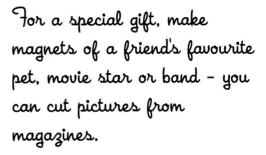

You're A Star!

Friends should always celebrate each other's strengths and talents.

Make special certificates for each other saying why each friend is so special, what she's really good at and why you love her.

This is to certify that

.... Minnie ....

is a fantastic friend!

She is *a great listener*

She is *always smiling*

She is *a great gal pal!*

Signed .... *Daisy x x* ....